AF234900

Impressum
Verlag: BABADADA GmbH, Nedderfeld 112 , 22529 Hamburg
Geschäftsführer / Verlagsleitung: Harald Hof
Druck: Books on Demand GmbH, In de Tarpen 42, 22848 Norderstedt

Imprint
Publisher: BABADADA GmbH, Nedderfeld 112 , 22529 Hamburg, Germany
Managing Director / Publishing direction: Harald Hof
Print: Books on Demand GmbH, In de Tarpen 42, 22848 Norderstedt

scol

school

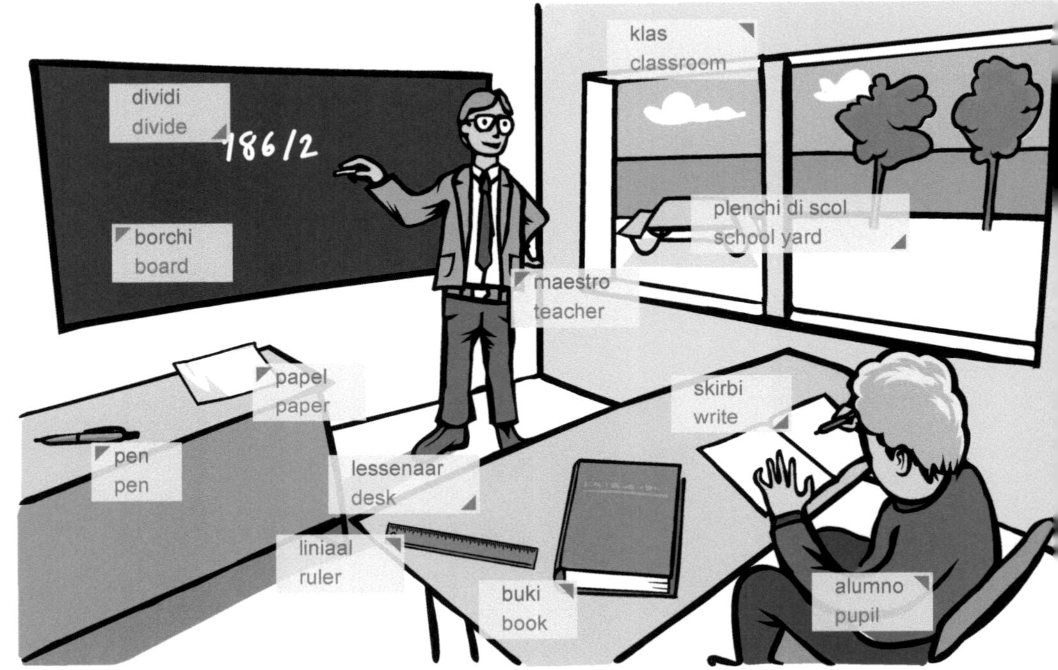

klas
classroom
dividi
divide
186/2
borchi
board
plenchi di scol
school yard
maestro
teacher
papel
paper
skirbi
write
pen
pen
lessenaar
desk
liniaal
ruler
buki
book
alumno
pupil

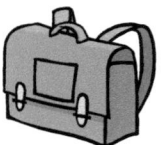

tas di scol

satchel

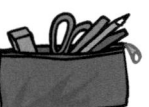

etui

pencil case

potlood

pencil

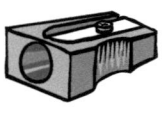

slijper

pencil sharpener

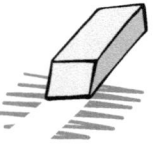

gum

rubber

buki di pinta

drawing pad

pintura

drawing

cuashi

paintbrush

caha di verf

paint box

sker

scissors

lijm

glue

schrift

exercise book

huiswerk

homework

number

number

suma

add

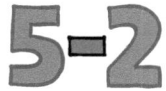

kita

subtract

multiplica

multiply

conta

calculate

letter

letter

alfabet

alphabet

palabra

word

texto

text

lesa

read

krijt

chalk

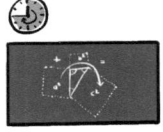

les

lesson

klassenboek

register

examen

examination

diploma

certificate

uniform di scol

school uniform

estudio

education

enciclopedia

encyclopedia

universidad

university

microscop

microscope

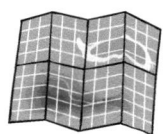

mapa

map

bari di sushi

waste-paper basket

biahamento
travel

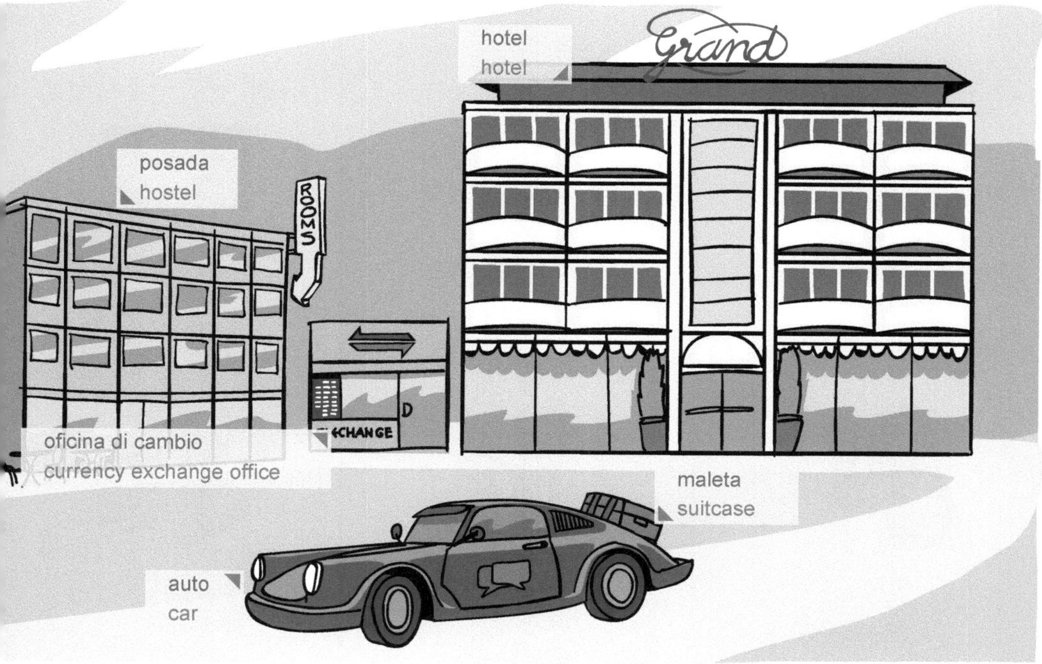

hotel
hotel
Grand
posada
hostel
ROOMS
EXCHANGE
oficina di cambio
currency exchange office
maleta
suitcase
auto
car

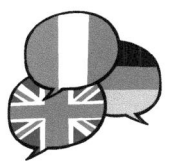

idioma

language

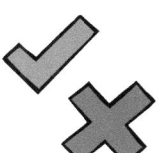

si / no

yes / no

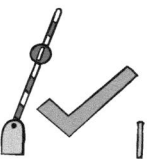

bon

Okay

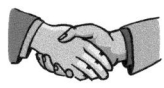

hallo

hello

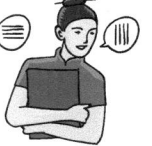

tolk

translator

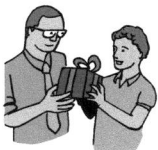

masha danki

Thank you

Cuanto esaki ta costa?

how much is…?

Mi no ta compronde

I don´t get it

problema

problem

bon nochi

Good evening!

Bon dia!

Good morning!

Bon nochi!

Good night!

ayo

goodbye

direccion

direction

maleta

luggage

handbag

bag

rugtas

backpack

huesped

guest

camber

room

slaapzak

sleeping bag

tent

tent

informacion pa turista

tourist information

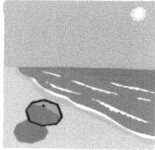

lama

beach

credit card

credit card

desayuno

breakfast

cuminda di merdia

lunch

cuminda di anochi

dinner

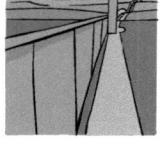

carchi

Ticket

cabe'i boto

elevator

stampia

stamp

grens

border

duana

customs

embahada

embassy

visa

visa

paspoort

passport

transport
transport

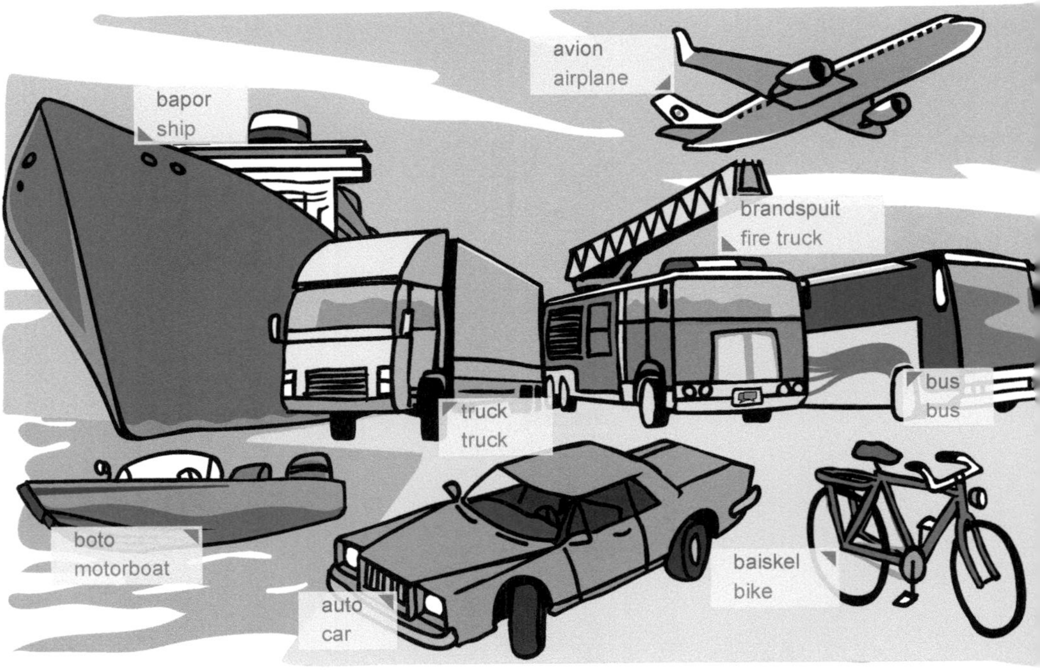
avion
airplane
bapor
ship
brandspuit
fire truck
bus
bus
truck
truck
boto
motorboat
baiskel
bike
auto
car

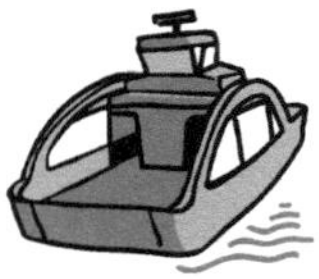

ferry
ferry

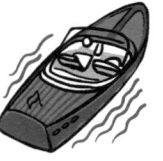

boto
boat

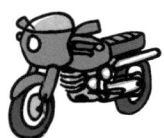

brommer
motorbike

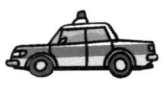

auto di polis
police car

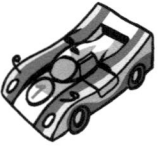

auto di careda
racing car

auto di huur
rental car

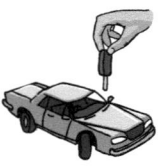

car sharing

car sharing

takelwagen

tow truck

dump truck

garbage truck

motor

engine

gasolin

fuel

pomp di gasolin

fuel station

borchi di trafico

traffic sign

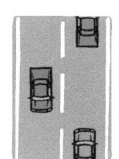

trafico

traffic

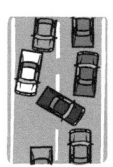

fila

traffic jam

parkeerplaats

parking lot

stacion di trein

train station

riel

tracks

trein

train

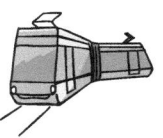

tram

tram

wagon

wagon

helicopter
helicopter

aeropuerto
airport

toren
tower

pasahero
passenger

container
container

caha di carton
carton

garoshi
cart

macutu
basket

lanta / baha
take off / land

ciudad

city

pueblo
village

centro di ciudad
city center

cas
house

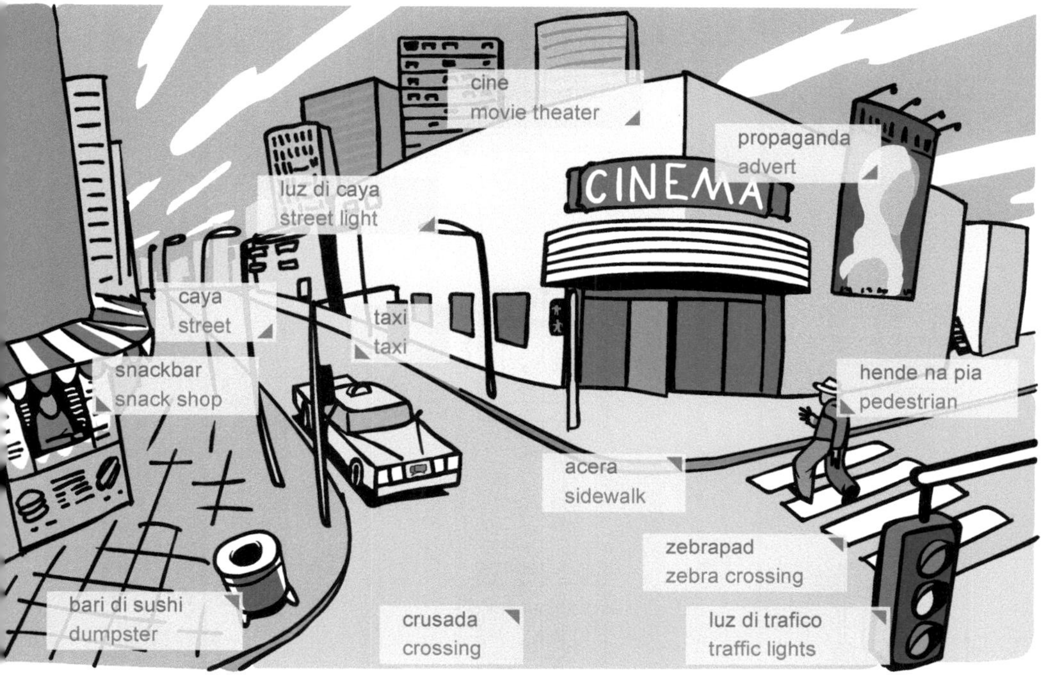
cine
movie theater
propaganda
advert
luz di caya
street light
CINEMA
caya
street
taxi
taxi
snackbar
snack shop
hende na pia
pedestrian
acera
sidewalk
zebrapad
zebra crossing
bari di sushi
dumpster
crusada
crossing
luz di trafico
traffic lights

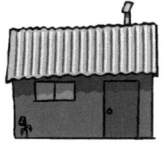

hut

hut

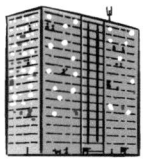

flat

apartment

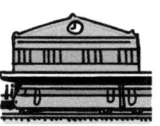

stacion di trein

train station

stadhuis

city hall

MUSEUM

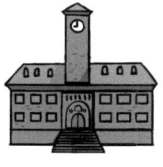

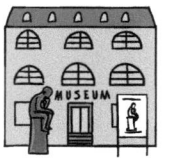

museo

museum

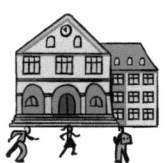

scol

school

universidad
university

banco
bank

hospital
hospital

hotel
hotel

botica
pharmacy

oficina
office

boekhandel
book shop

tienda
shop

floresteria
flower shop

supermarket
supermarket

mercado
market

department store
department store

bendedo di pisca
fishmonger's shop

shopping center
mall

haf
harbor

park
park

banki
bench

brug
bridge

trapi
stairs

metro
subway

tunnel
tunnel

parada di bus
bus stop

bar
bar

restaurant
restaurant

postbox
postbox

borchi di nomber di caya
street sign

parkeermeter
parking meter

parke di bestia
zoo

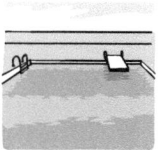

piscina
swimming pool

moskee
mosque

cunucu
farm

polucion
pollution

santana
cemetery

misa
church

speelplaats
playground

tempel
temple

paisahe
landscape

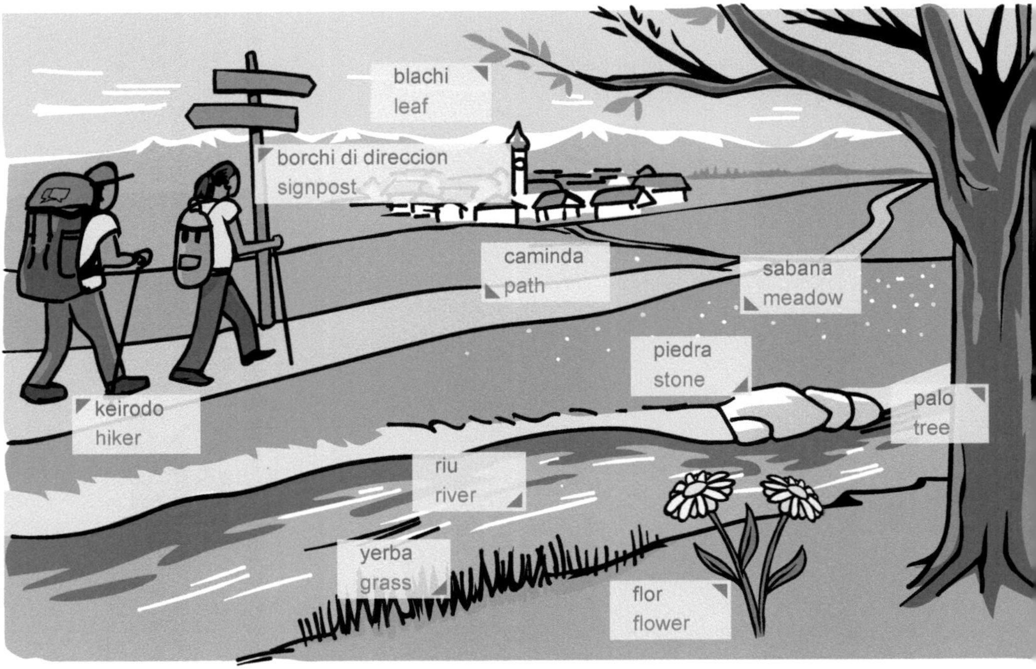

blachi
leaf

borchi di direccion
signpost

caminda
path

sabana
meadow

piedra
stone

palo
tree

keirodo
hiker

riu
river

yerba
grass

flor
flower

vallei
valley

sero
hill

lago
lake

mondi
forest

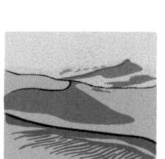

desierto
desert

volcan
volcano

kasteel
castle

arco iris
rainbow

paddenstoel
mushroom

palma
palm tree

sangura
mosquito

musca
fly

vruminga
ant

bij
bee

haraña
spider

tor

beetle

dori

frog

eekhoorn

squirrel

porcospina

hedgehog

coneu

hare

shoco

owl

parha

bird

zwaan

swan

porco di mondi

boar

bina

deer

eland

moose

dam

dam

molina di biento

wind turbine

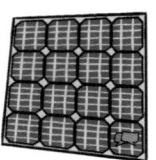

panel solar

solar panel

clima

climate

paisahe - landscape

restaurant
restaurant

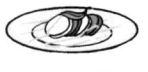

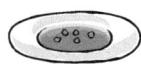

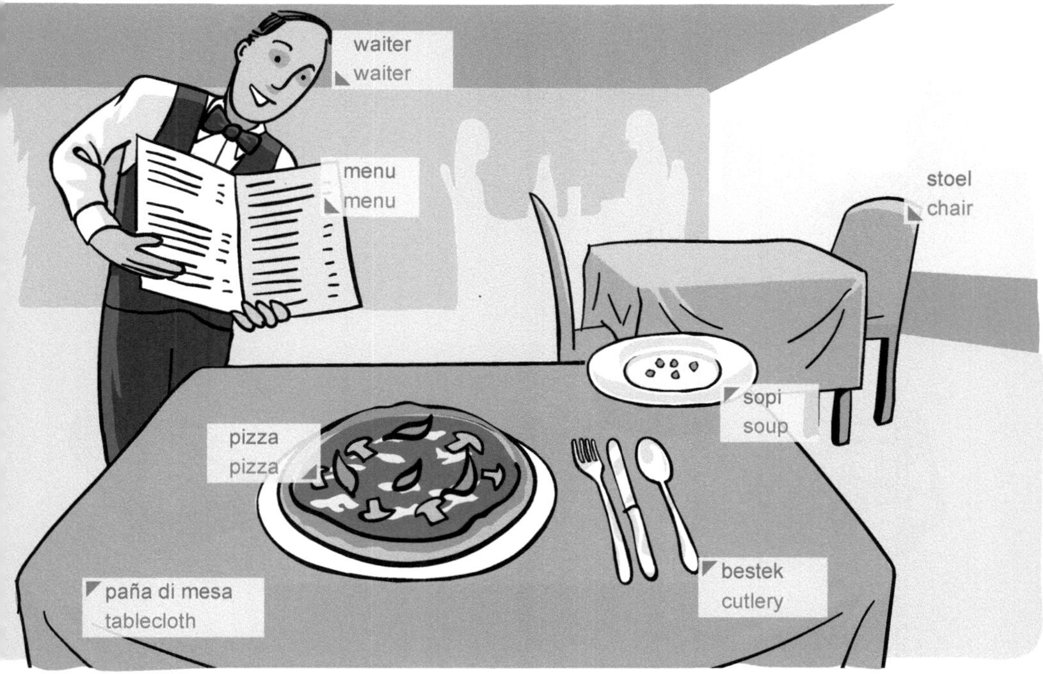
waiter
waiter
menu
menu
stoel
chair
sopi
soup
pizza
pizza
bestek
cutlery
paña di mesa
tablecloth

aperitivo

starter

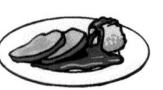

cuminda principal

main course

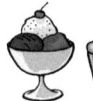

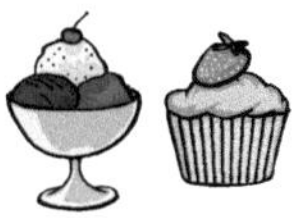

dessert

dessert

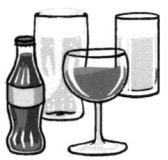

bebida

drinks

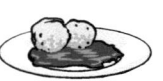

cuminda

food

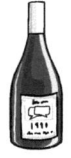

boter

bottle

fastfood

fast food

streetfood

street food

canica di te

teapot

pochi di sucu

sugar bowl

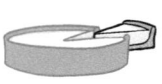

porcion

portion

espressomachine

espresso machine

stoel di mucha

high chair

cuenta

bill

hasechi

tray

cuchiu

knife

forki

fork

cuchara

spoon

telep

teaspoon

napkin

serviette

glas

glass

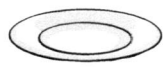

tayo
plate

tayo di sopi
soup plate

scoter
saucer

saus
sauce

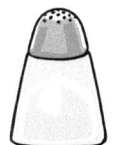

pochi di salo
salt shaker

mulina di peper
pepper mill

binager
vinegar

azeta
oil

specerij
spices

ketchup
ketchup

mosterd
mustard

mayonaise
mayonnaise

supermarket
supermarket

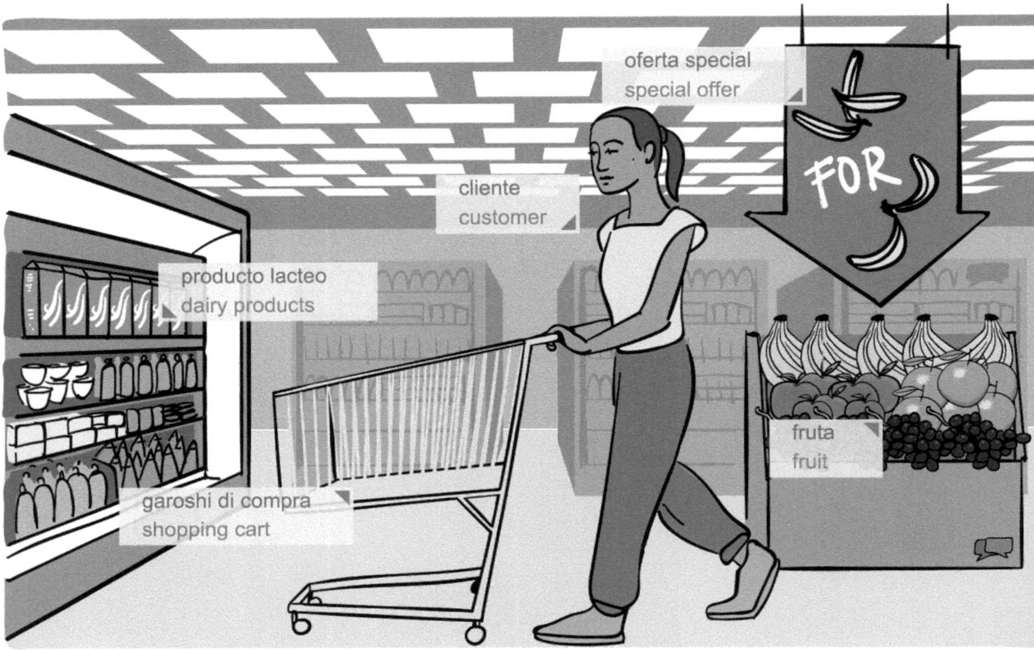
oferta special
special offer
FOR
cliente
customer
producto lacteo
dairy products
fruta
fruit
garoshi di compra
shopping cart

BUTCHERS

carniceria

butcher's shop

BAKERY

panaderia

bakery

pisa

weigh

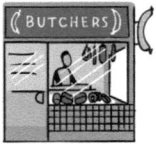

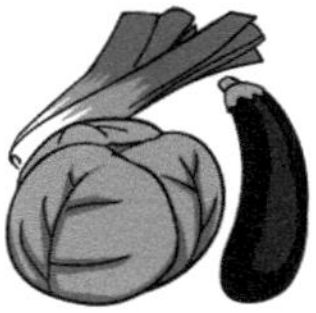

berdura

vegetables

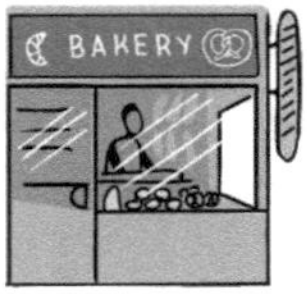

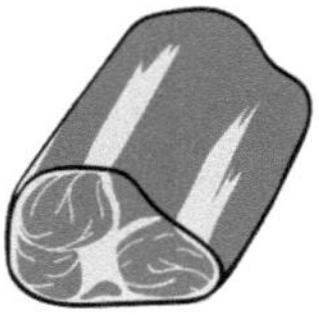

carni

meat

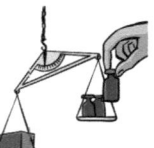

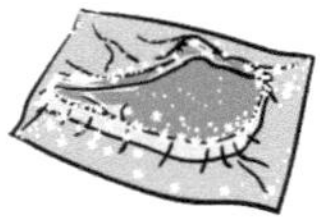

frozen food

frozen food

beleg di carni
cold cuts

cuminda di bleki
canned food

detergente na puiro
detergent

mangel
candy

producto pa cas
household products

articulo di limpiesa
cleaning products

bendedo
sales representative

cahero
cash register

cahero
cashier

lista di compra
shopping list

orario
opening hours

cartera
wallet

credit card
credit card

tas
bag

saco di plastic
plastic bag

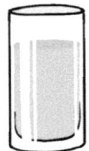

awa

water

juice

juice

lechi

milk

cola

coke

biña

wine

cerbes

beer

alcohol

alcohol

chocomel

cocoa

te

tea

koffie

coffee

espresso

espresso

cappuccino

cappuccino

bacoba

banana

appel

apple

apelsina

orange

milon

melon

lamunchi

lemon

wortel

carrot

conoflok

garlic

bambu

bamboo

siboyo

onion

mushroom

mushroom

noot

nuts

pasta

noodles

spaghetti
spaghetti

aros
rice

salada
salad

batata hasa
fries

batata hasa
fried potatoes

pizza
pizza

hamburger
hamburger

sandwich
sandwich

cutlet
escalope

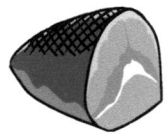

ham
ham

salami
salami

soseishi
sausage

galiña
chicken

hasa
roast

pisca
fish

cuminda - food

papa

porridge oats

müsli

muesli

cornflakes

cornflakes

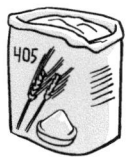

hariña

flour

croissant

croissant

pan rondo

bread roll

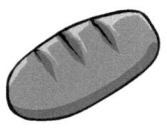

pan

bread

toast

toast

cuki

cookies

manteca

butter

kwark

curd

bolo

cake

webo

egg

webo hasa

fried egg

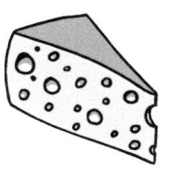

keshi

cheese

ijscream

ice cream

sucu

sugar

honing

honey

jam

jelly

pasta di chuculati

nougat cream

curry

curry

cunucu

farm

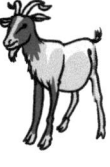

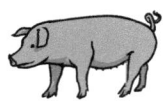

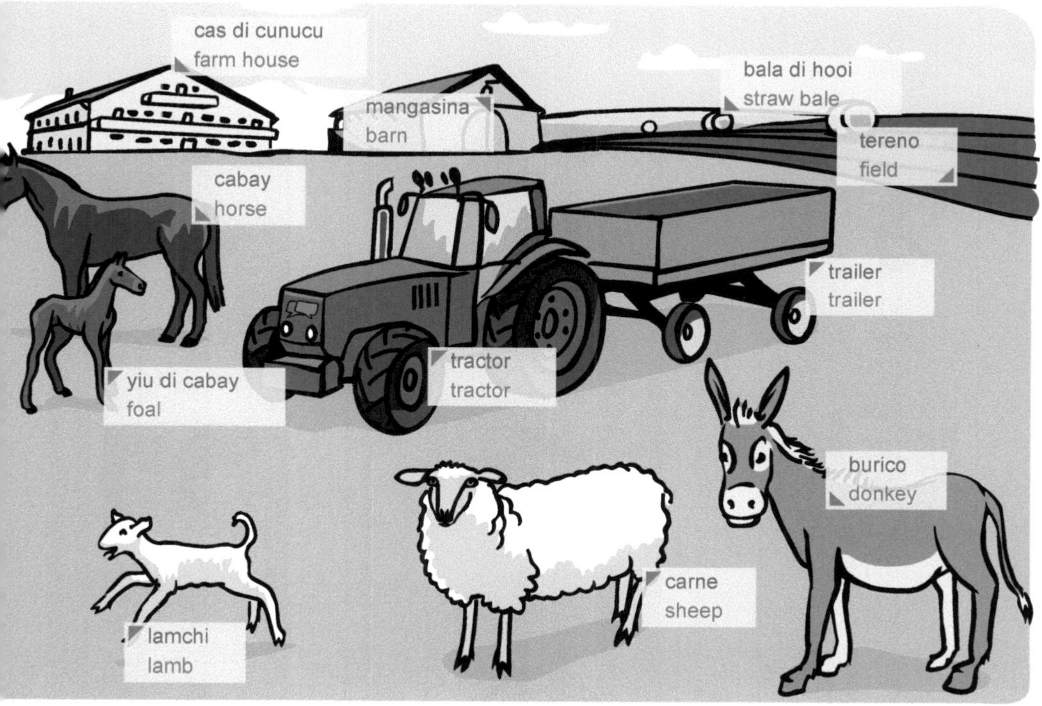
cas di cunucu
farm house
mangasina
barn
bala di hooi
straw bale
tereno
field
cabay
horse
trailer
trailer
tractor
tractor
yiu di cabay
foal
burico
donkey
carne
sheep
lamchi
lamb

cabrito

goat

baca

cow

bishe

calf

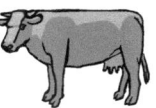

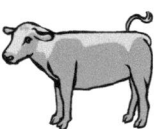

porco

pig

yiu di porco

piglet

toro

bull

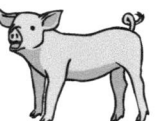

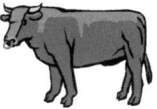

gans

goose

pato

duck

puyito

chick

galiña

hen

gay

cockerel

djaca

rat

pushi

cat

raton

mouse

toro

ox

cacho

dog

cas di cacho

dog house

slang pa muha mata

garden hose

gieter

watering can

herment pa corta yerbe

scythe

ploeg

plow

garabati

sickle

chapi

hoe

forki pa coy hooi

pitchfork

hacha

axe

garetia

pushcart

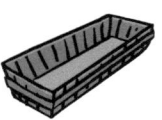

pesebre

trough

canica di lechi

milk can

saco

sack

heki

fence

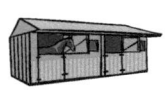

stal

stable

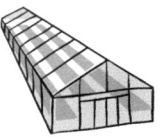

greenhouse

greenhouse

suela

soil

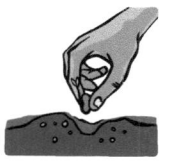

simia

seed

mest

fertilizer

mashin di cosecha

combine harvester

cosecha

harvest

cosecha

harvest

yams

yams

trigo

wheat

soya

soya

batata

potato

maishi

corn

canola

rapeseed

palo di fruta

fruit tree

yuca

manioc

grano

grain

cas

house

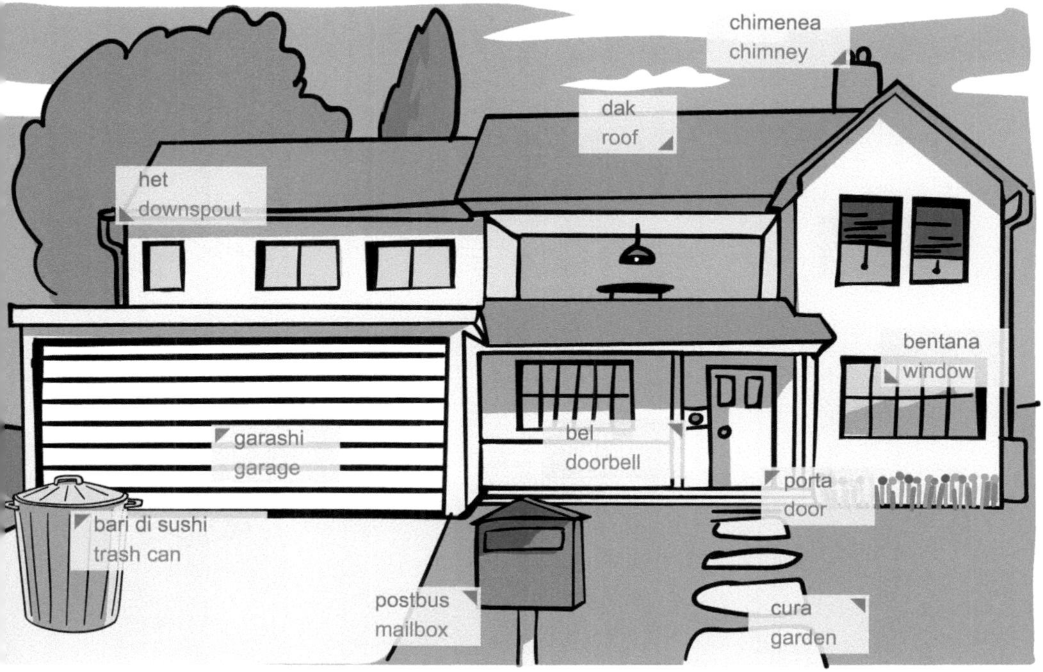

chimenea
chimney
dak
roof
het
downspout
bentana
window
garashi
garage
bel
doorbell
porta
door
bari di sushi
trash can
postbus
mailbox
cura
garden

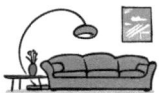

sala

living room

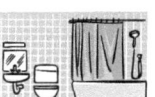

baño

bathroom

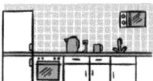

cushina

kitchen

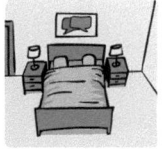

camber

bedroom

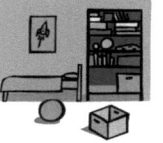

camber di mucha

kids room

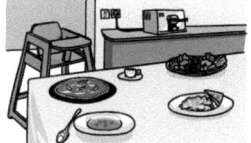

comedo

dining room

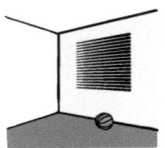

suela

floor

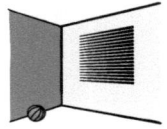

muraya

wall

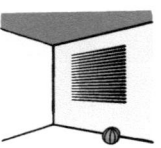

blafon

ceiling

bodega

cellar

sauna

sauna

balcon

balcony

terasa

terrace

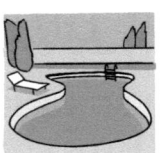

piscina

pool

mashin di corta yerba

lawn mower

laken

sheet

bedsprei

bedspread

cama

bed

basora

broom

hemchi

bucket

switch

switch

sala

living room

papel pa papela
wallpaper
potret
picture
lampi
lamp
reki
shelf
cashi
cabinet
television
television
fogon
fireplace
flor
flower
cusinchi
cushion
sofa
sofa
vaas
vase
remote control
remote control

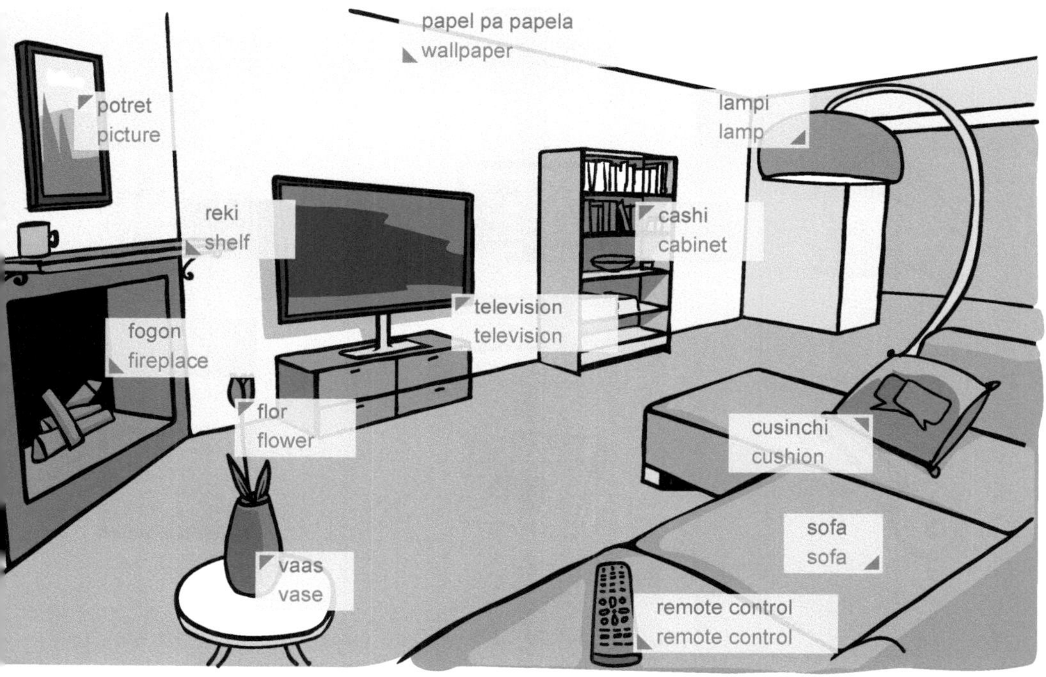

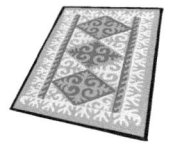

tapijt

carpet

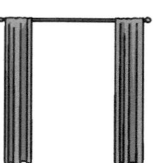

cortina

drape

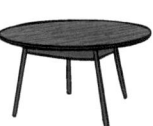

mesa

table

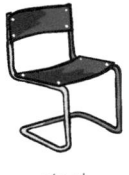

stoel

chair

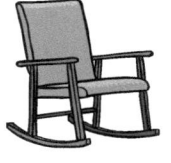

stoel di zoya

rocking chair

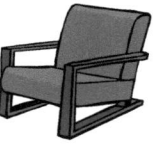

stoel

armchair

buki

book

dekel

blanket

decoracion

decoration

palo pa kima

firewood

film

film

stereoset

stereo system

yabi

key

corant

newspaper

cuadra

painting

poster

poster

radio

radio

blocnote

notebook

stofzuiger

vacuum cleaner

cadushi

cactus

bela

candle

cushina
kitchen

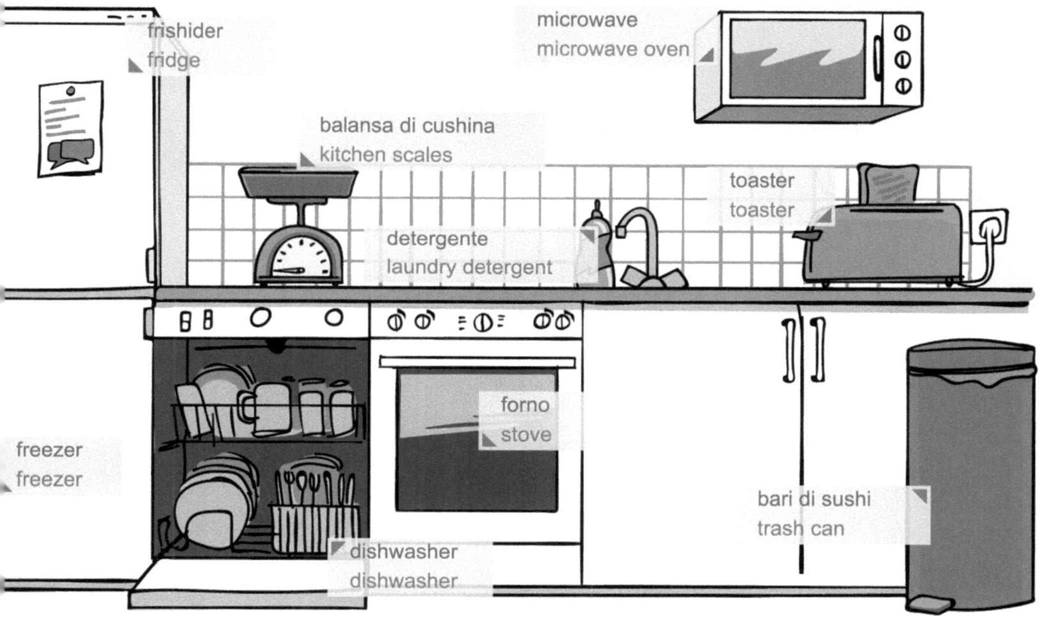
frishider
fridge
microwave
microwave oven
balansa di cushina
kitchen scales
toaster
toaster
detergente
laundry detergent
forno
stove
freezer
freezer
bari di sushi
trash can
dishwasher
dishwasher

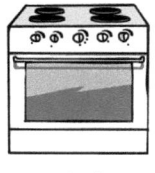

stoof
cooker

wea
pot

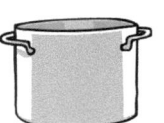

wea di hero
cast-iron pot

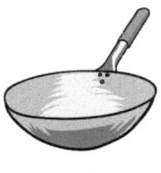

wok
wok / kadai

planchi
pan

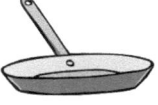

ketel
kettle

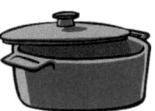

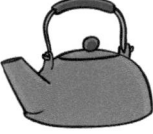

steamer

steamer

teblachi pa horna

baking tray

servies

crockery

beker

mug

conchi

bowl

chopstick

chopsticks

cuchara di sopi

ladle

spatula

spatula

garde

whisk

scurido

strainer

colado

sieve

raspa

grater

fenso

mortar

barbecue

barbecue

candela

fireplace

planki pa corta

chopping board

rostok

rolling pin

kurkentrek

corkscrew

bleki

can

cos di habri bleki

can opener

pannenlap

oven cloth

wasbak

sink

skeiro

brush

spons

sponge

blender

blender

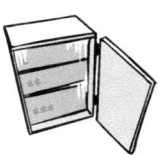

freezer

deep freezer

tetero

baby bottle

cranchi

tap

baño

bathroom

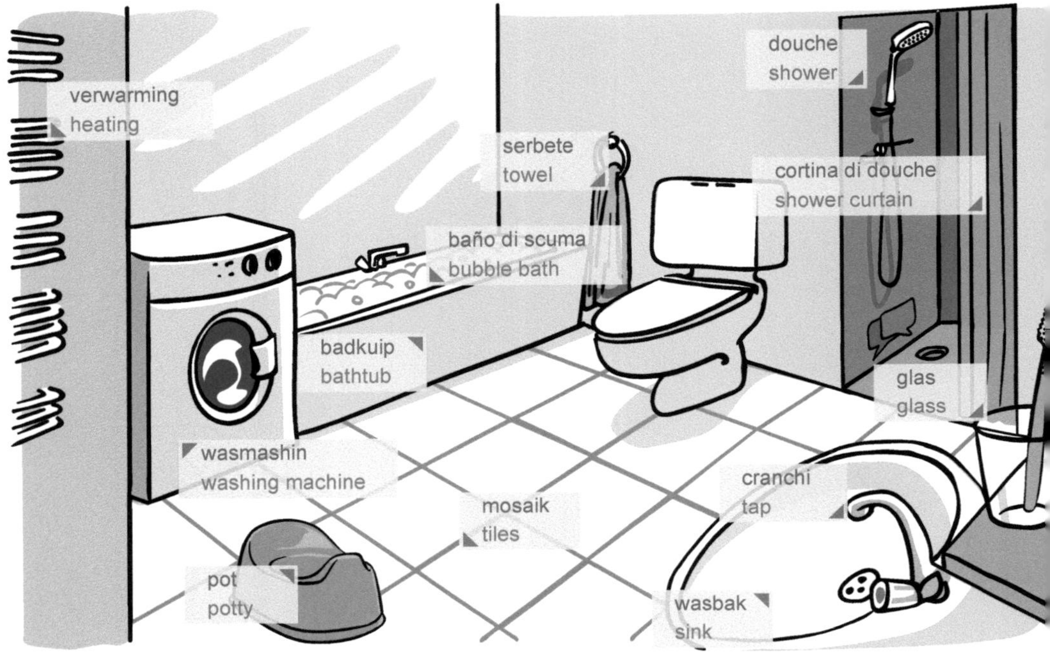

verwarming
heating
serbete
towel
douche
shower
cortina di douche
shower curtain
baño di scuma
bubble bath
badkuip
bathtub
glas
glass
wasmashin
washing machine
cranchi
tap
mosaik
tiles
pot
potty
wasbak
sink

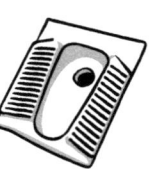

tualet

toilet

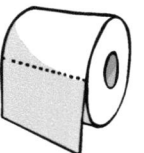

hurktoilet

squat toilet

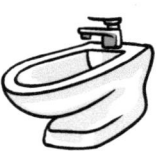

bidet

bidet

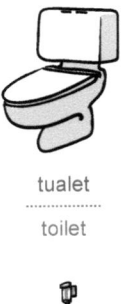

urinal

urinal

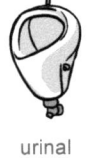

papel di w.c.

toilet paper

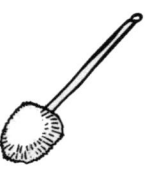

skeiro di w.c.

toilet brush

skeiro di djente

toothbrush

pasta di djente

toothpaste

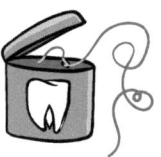

dental floss

dental floss

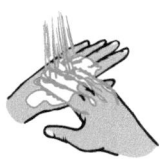

laba

wash

douche di man

hand shower

bidet

douche

tobo

basin

skeiro

back brush

habon

soap

shower gel

shower gel

shampoo

shampoo

washandje

flannel

drain

drain

crema

creme

desodorante

deodorant

spiel

mirror

spiel di man

hand mirror

blet

razor

shaving foam

shaving foam

aftershave

aftershave

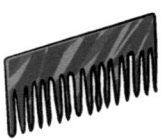

peña

comb

skeiro

brush

blower

hair-dryer

spray pa cabey

hairspray

makeup

makeup

lipstick

lipstick

cos di pinta huña

nail varnish

catuna

cotton wool

sker pa corta huña

nail scissors

perfume

perfume

tas
washbag

kruk
stool

balansa
weighing scales

bata
bathrobe

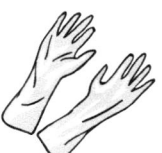

handschoen
rubber gloves

tampon
tampon

kotex
sanitary towel

wc kimico
chemical toilet

camber di mucha
kids room

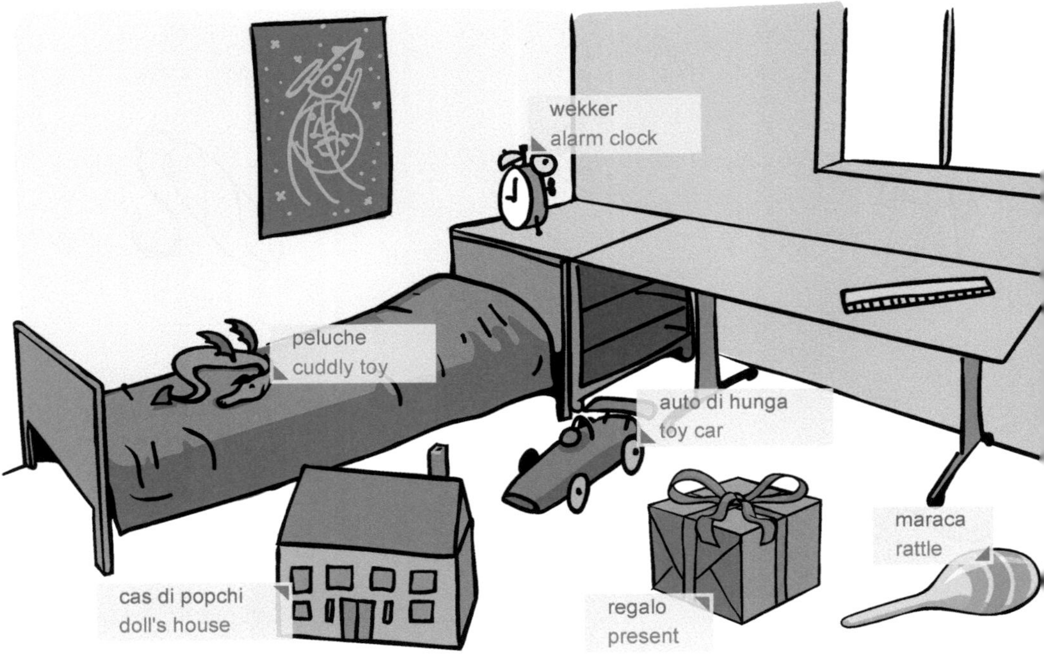

wekker
alarm clock
peluche
cuddly toy
auto di hunga
toy car
maraca
rattle
cas di popchi
doll's house
regalo
present

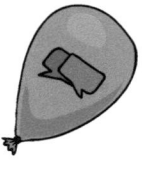

blaas
balloon

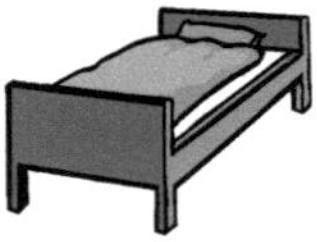

cama
bed

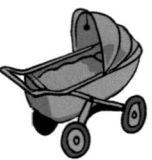

stroller
stroller

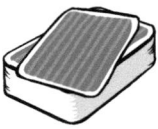

baraha di carta
deck of cards

puzzel
jigsaw

SUPER MEGA

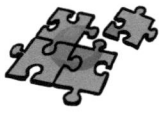

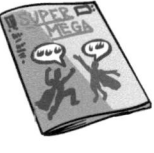

comic
comic

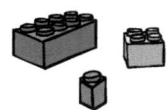

lego

lego bricks

bloki di hunga

toy blocks

figura di accion

action figure

romper

romper suit

frisbee

frisbee

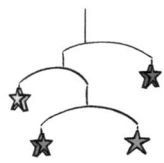

mobil

mobile

wega di mesa

board game

dou

dice

set di trein

model train set

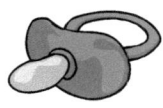

chupon

pacifier

fiesta

party

buki di prenchi

picture book

bala

ball

popchi

doll

hunga

play

zandbak

sandpit

zoya

swing

cos di hunga

toys

videogame

video game console

tricycle

tricycle

beer

teddy bear

cashi di paña

wardrobe

paña
clothing

mea

socks

mea

stockings

pantyhose

tights

sjaal
scarf

paraplu
umbrella

faha
belt

T-shirt
t-shirt

boots
boots

slof
slippers

keds
sneakers

sandalia
sandals

sapato
shoes

laars di rubber
rubber boots

carsonsio
underwear

bh
bra

flanel
undershirt

body
body

carson
pants

jeans
jeans

saya
skirt

blusa
blouse

camisa
shirt

sweater
pullover

sweater
sweater

blazer
blazer

jacket
jacket

jas
coat

regenjas
raincoat

flus
costume

shimis
dress

shimis di bruid
wedding dress

flus
suit

yapon
nightgown

pidjama
pajamas

sari
sari

lenso di cabes
headscarf

turban
turban

burqa
burka

kaftan
kaftan

abaya
abaya

zwempak
swimsuit

zwembroek
trunks

carson cortico
shorts

trainingspak
tracksuit

lantera
apron

handschoen
gloves

boton
button

bril
glasses

armband
bracelet

cadena
necklace

renchi
ring

renchi di horea
earring

pechi
cap

kapstok
coat hanger

sombre
hat

dashi
tie

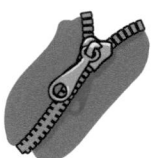

ziper
zip

helm
helmet

guiel
braces

uniform di scol
school uniform

uniform
uniform

babado

bib

chupon

pacifier

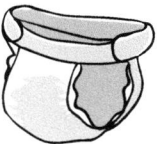

bruki

diaper

oficina
office

filekast
filing cabinet

server
server

papel
paper

printer
printer

pantaya
monitor

lessenaar
desk

mouse
mouse

map
folder

keyboard
keyboard

bari di sushi
waste-paper basket

computer
computer

stoel
chair

copi pa bebe koffie

coffee mug

calculator

calculator

internet

internet

laptop

laptop

carta

letter

mensahe

message

celular

cell phone

red

network

mashin di copia

photocopier

software

software

telefon

telephone

stopcontact

plug socket

fax mashin

fax machine

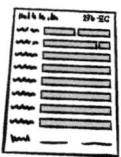

formulario

form

documento

document

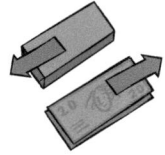

cumpra

buy

paga

pay

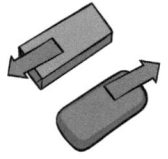

negosha

trade

placa

money

 USD

dollar

dollar

 EUR

euro

euro

 JPY

yen

yen

 RUB

roebel

rouble

 CHF

frank suiso

Swiss franc

 CNY

yuan renminbi

renminbi yuan

 INR

roepi

rupee

bancomatico

cash point

oficina di cambio

currency exchange office

oro

gold

plata

silver

azeta

oil

energia

energy

prijs

price

contract

contract

impuesto

tax

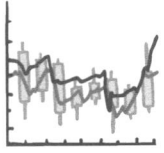

share

stock

traha

work

empleado

employee

dunado di trabou

employer

fabrica

factory

tienda

shop

ofishi / profesion
occupations

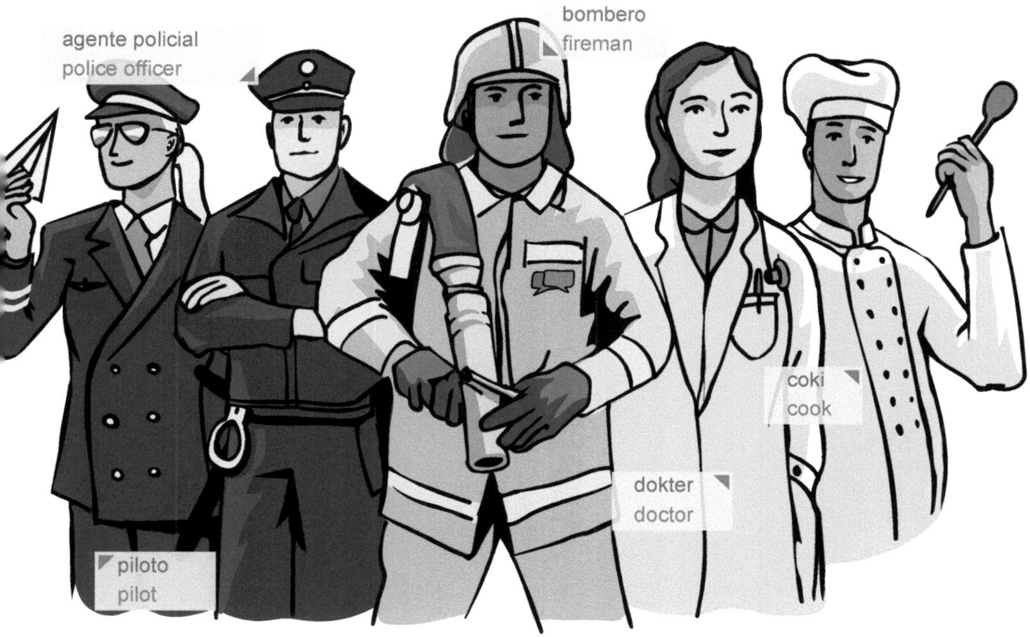

agente policial
police officer
bombero
fireman
coki
cook
dokter
doctor
piloto
pilot

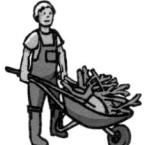

hardinero

gardener

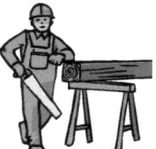

carpinte

carpenter

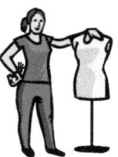

cosedo

seamstress

hues

judge

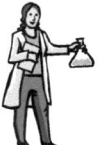

kimico

chemist

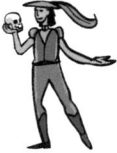

actor

actor

chauffeur di bus

bus driver

chauffeur di taxi

taxi driver

piscado

fisherman

hende cu ta haci cas limpi

cleaning lady

drechado di dak

roofer

waiter

waiter

jaagdo

hunter

verfdo

painter

panadero

baker

electricista

electrician

trahado den construccion

builder

ingeniero

engineer

carnicero

butcher

loodgieter

plumber

partido di carta

postman

solda

soldier

arkitecto

architect

cahero

cashier

florista

florist

pelukero / pelukera

hairdresser

controlado di ticket

conductor

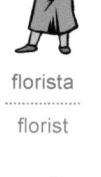

mecanico

mechanic

capitan

captain

dentista

dentist

cientifico

scientist

rabbi

rabbi

imam

imam

monk

monk

pastor

pastor

herment
tools

martiu
hammer
pins
pliers
schroefdraai
screwdriver
flashlight
torch
wrench
wrench

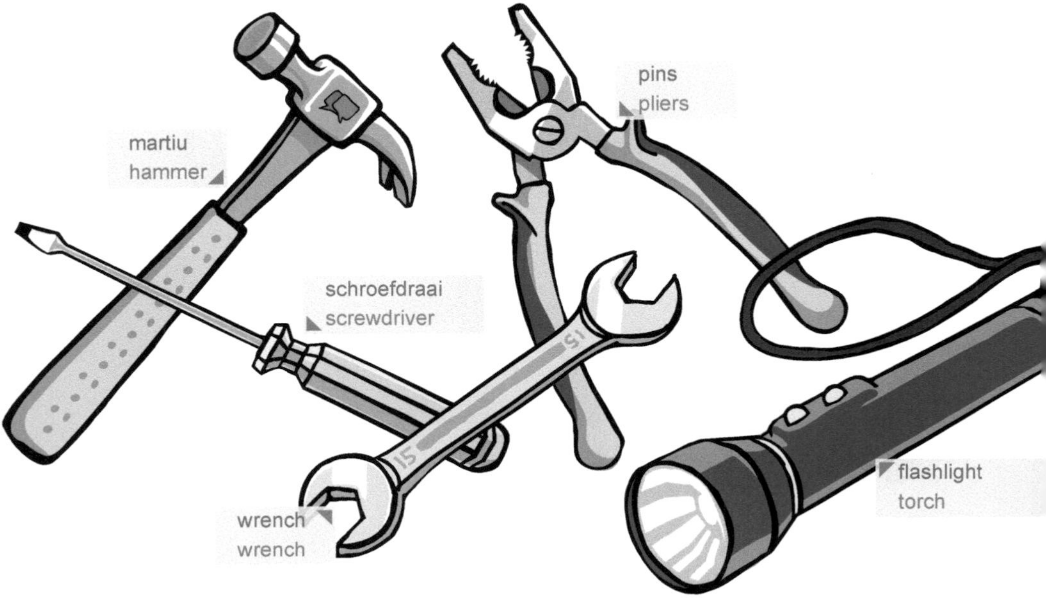

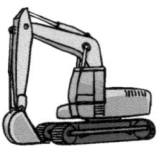

bulldozer

excavator

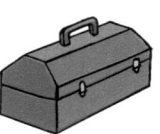

caha di herment

toolbox

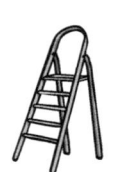

trapi

ladder

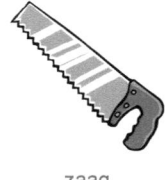

zaag

saw

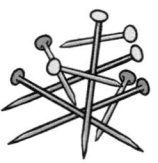

clabo

nails

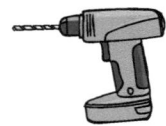

boormashin

drill

drecha
....
repair

shobel
....
shovel

caraho!
....
Damn!

scop
....
dustpan

bleki di verf
....
paint can

schroef
....
screws

instrumento musical
musical instruments

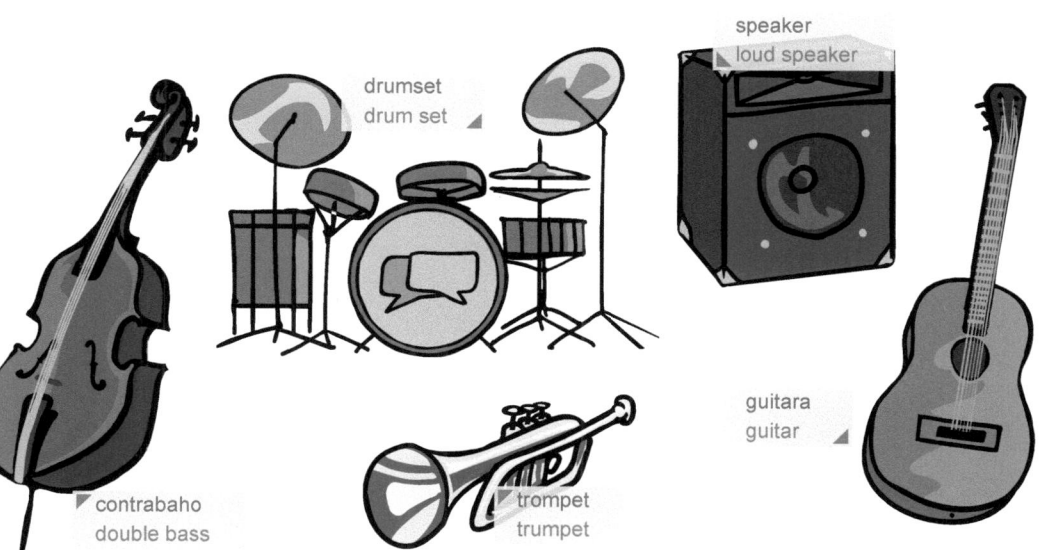

drumset
drum set

speaker
loud speaker

guitara
guitar

contrabaho
double bass

trompet
trumpet

piano

piano

fio

violin

baho

bass

timbal

timpani

tambu

drums

keyboard

keyboard

saxofon

saxophone

fluit

flute

microfon

microphone

parke di bestia

zoo

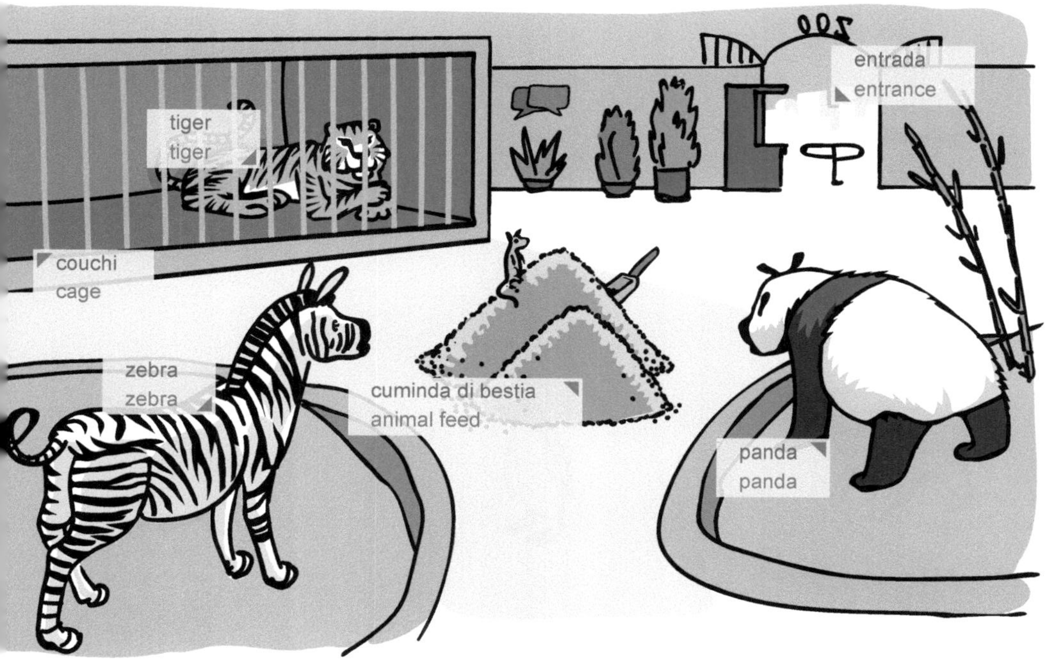

tiger
tiger
entrada
entrance
couchi
cage
zebra
zebra
cuminda di bestia
animal feed
panda
panda

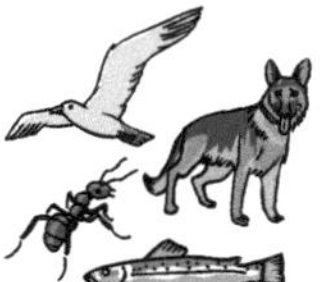

animal
animals

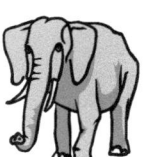

olifante
elephant

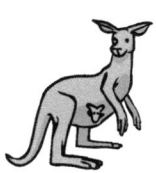

cangaru
kangaroo

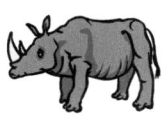

neushoorn
rhino

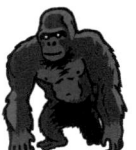

gorila
gorilla

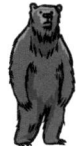

beer
bear

camel

camel

avestruz

ostrich

leon

lion

macaco

monkey

flamingo

flamingo

lora

parrot

beer polar

polar bear

pinguin

penguin

tribon

shark

pauwies

peacock

colebra

snake

caiman

crocodile

cuidado di bestia

zookeeper

cacho di awa

seal

jaguar

jaguar

pony

pony

leopardo

leopard

hipopotamo

hippo

giraf

giraffe

aguila

eagle

porco di mondi

boar

pisca

fish

turtuga

turtle

walrus

walrus

vos

fox

gazelle

gazelle

futbol Americano
American football

ciclismo
cycling

tennis
tennis

basketball
basketball

landamento
swimming

boxeo
boxing

ice hockey
ice hockey

futbol
soccer

badminton
badminton

atletismo
athletics

handbal
handball

ski
skiing

polo
polo

hari
laugh

bula
jump

brasa
hug

cana
walk

canta
sing

soña
dream

resa
pray

sunchi
kiss

skirbi
write

pinta
draw

mustra
show

primi
push

duna
give

coy
take

tin

have

haci

do

ta

be

para

stand

core

run

ranca

pull

tira

throw

cay

fall

drumi

lie

warda

wait

carga

carry

sinta

sit

bisti

get dressed

drumi

sleep

lanta fo'i soño

wake up

mira

look at

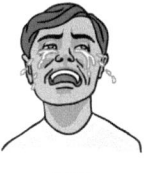

yora

cry

caricia

stroke

peña

comb

papia

talk

compronde

understand

puntra

ask

scucha

listen

bebe

drink

come

eat

ruim op

tidy up

stima

love

cushna

cook

bai

drive

bula

fly

zeilo

sail

conta

calculate

lesa

read

siña

learn

traha

work

casa

marry

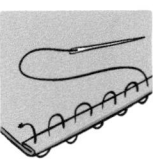

cose

sew

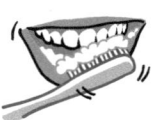

skeiro djente

brush teeth

mata

kill

huma

smoke

manda

send

wela
grandmother

welo
grandfather

tata
father

mama
mother

baby
baby

yiu muhe
daughter

yiu homber
son

huesped

guest

tanta

aunt

omo

uncle

ruman homber

brother

ruman muhe

sister

curpa

body

frenta
forehead
wowo
eye
schouder
shoulder
dede
finger
cara
face
cachete
chin
man
hand
pia
leg
pecho
breast
brasa
arm

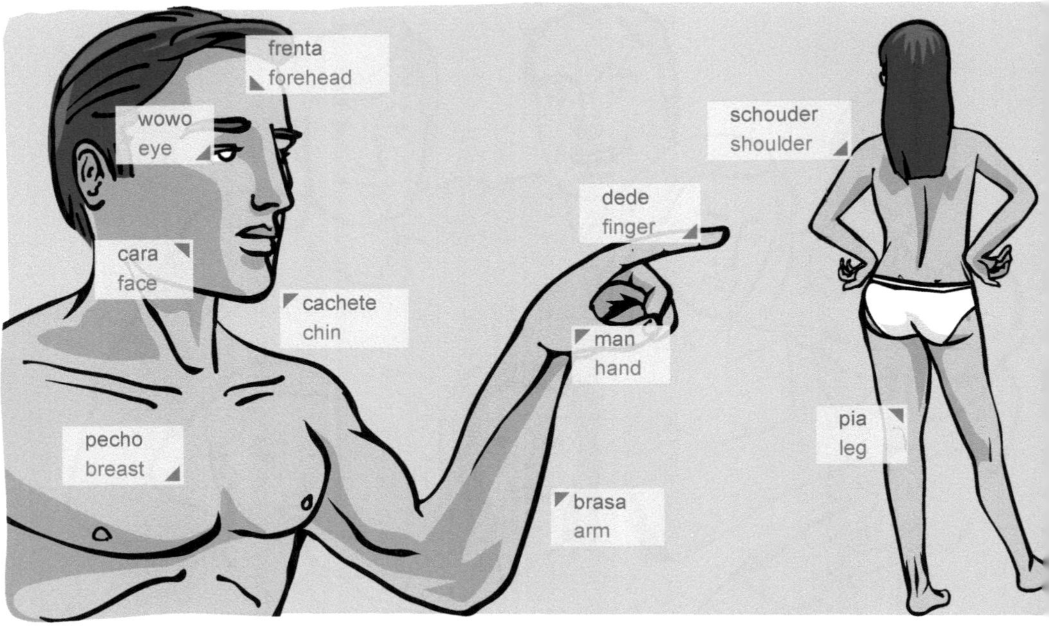

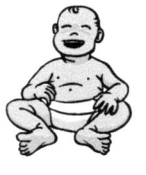

baby

baby

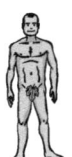

homber

man

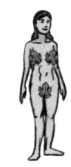

muhe

woman

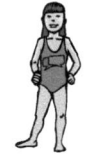

mucha muhe

girl

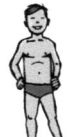

mucha homber

boy

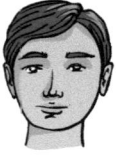

cabes

head

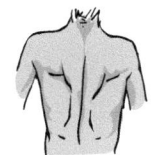

lomba

back

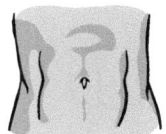

bariga

belly

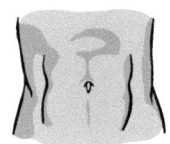

lombrishi

navel

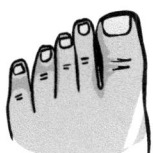

dede di pia

toe

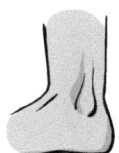

hilchi

heel

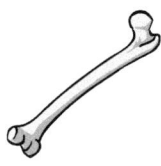

weso

bone

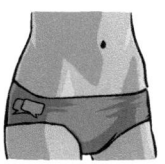

heup

hip

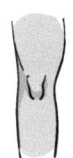

rudia

knee

elleboog

elbow

nanishi

nose

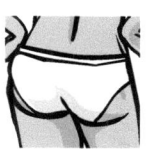

chanchan

buttocks

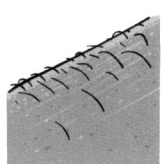

cuero

skin

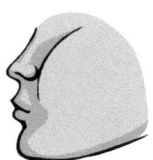

wang

cheek

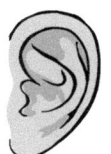

horea

ear

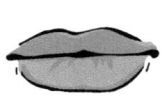

lip

lip

boca

mouth

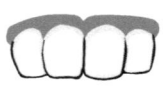

djente

tooth

lenga

tongue

celebro

brain

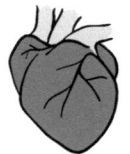

curason

heart

musculo

muscle

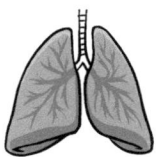

pulmon

lung

higra

liver

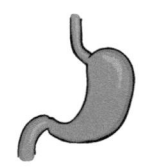

stoma

stomach

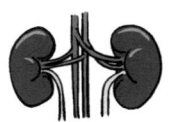

nier

kidneys

sex

sex

condon

condom

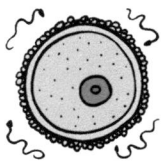

ovulo

ovum

sperma

semen

embaraso

pregnancy

curpa - body

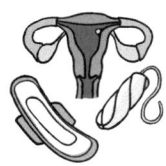

menstruacion

menstruation

vagina

vagina

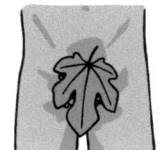

penis

penis

wenkbrauw

eyebrow

cabey

hair

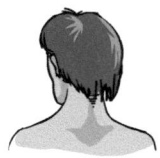

nek

neck

hospital
hospital

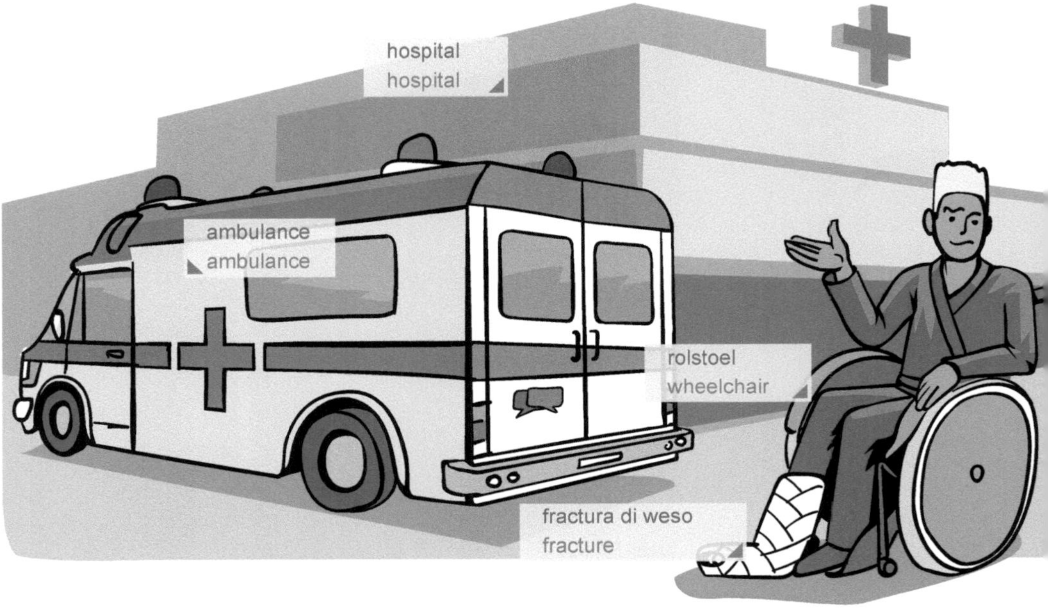

hospital
hospital
ambulance
ambulance
rolstoel
wheelchair
fractura di weso
fracture

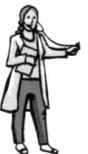

dokter

doctor

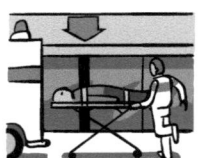

EHBO (prome asistencia/eerste hulp)

emergency room

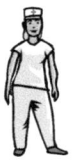

nurse

nurse

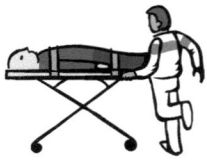

caso di emergencia

emergency

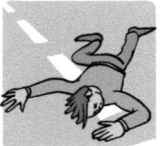

fo'i tino

unconscious

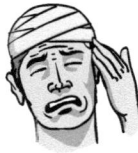

dolor

pain

lesion
injury

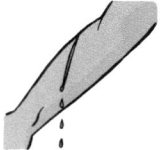

sangramento
bleeding

ataca di curason
heart attack

ataca celebral
stroke

alergia
allergy

tosa
cough

keintura
fever

griep
flu

diarea
diarrhea

dolor di cabes
headache

cancer
cancer

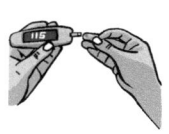

diabetes
diabetes

ciruhano
surgeon

scalpel
scalpel

operacion
operation

CT
·········
CT

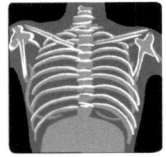

x-ray
·········
x-ray

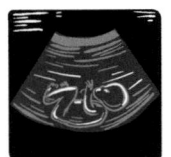

echo
·········
ultrasound

masker contra stof
·········
face mask

malesa
·········
disease

sala di espera
·········
waiting room

kruk
·········
crutch

pleister
·········
plaster

verband
·········
bandage

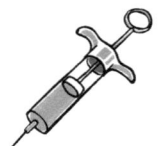

inyeccion
·········
injection

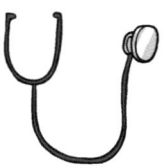

stetoscop
·········
stethoscope

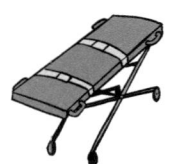

brancard
·········
stretcher

thermometer
·········
clinical thermometer

nacemento
·········
birth

sobrepeso
·········
overweight

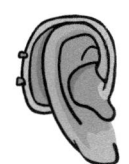

aparato pa oido

hearing aid

desinfectante

disinfectant

infeccion

infection

virus

virus

HIV / AIDS

HIV / AIDS

remedi

medicine

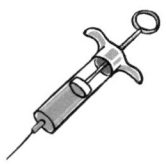

vacuna

vaccination

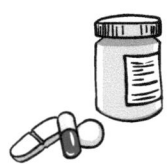

pilder

tablets

pilder

pill

yamada di emergencia

emergency call

aparato pa midi presion

blood pressure monitor

malo / saludabel

ill / healthy

auxilio!

Help!

alarma

alarm

atraco

assault

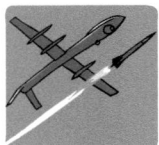

atake

attack

peliger

danger

salida di emergencia

emergency exit

candela

Fire!

brandspuit

fire extinguisher

desgracia

accident

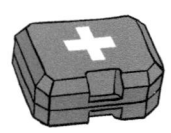

caha di prome asistencia

first-aid kit

SOS

SOS

polis

police

Europa

Europe

Noord America

North America

Sur America

South America

Africa

Africa

Asia

Asia

Australia

Australia

Oceano Atlantico

Atlantic

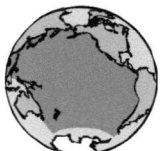

Oceano Pacifico

Pacific

Oceano Indio

Indian Ocean

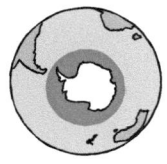

Oceano Antartico

Antarctic Ocean

Oceano Artico

Arctic Ocean

Noordpool

North pole

Zuidpool

South pole

Antartica

Antarctica

mundo

earth

tera

land

lama

sea

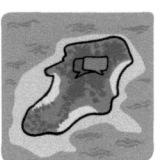

isla

island

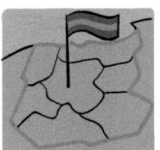

nacion

nation

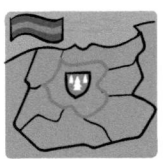

estado

state

holoshi analog

clock face

wijzer chikito

hour hand

wijzer grandi

minute hand

wijzer di seconde

second hand

Cuant'or tin?

What time is it?

dia

day

tempo

time

awor

now

holoshi digital

digital watch

minuut

minute

ora

hour

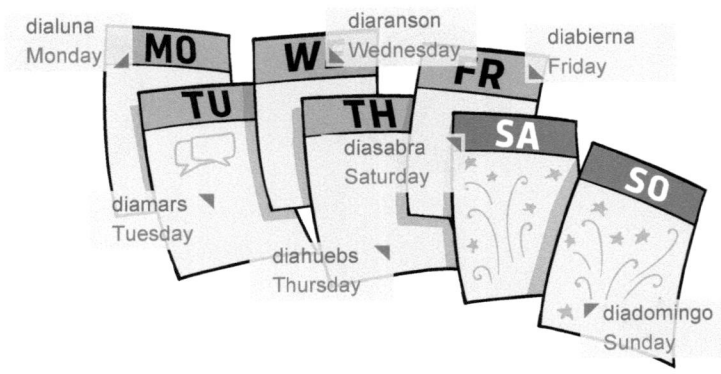

dialuna — Monday — MO
diaranson — Wednesday — W
diabierna — Friday — FR
TU
TH
SA
diamars — Tuesday
diasabra — Saturday
diahuebs — Thursday
SO
diadomingo — Sunday

ayera

yesterday

awe

today

mañan

tomorrow

mainta

morning

merdia

noon

anochi

evening

MO	TU	WE	TH	FR	SA	SU
1	2	3	4	5	6	7
8	9	10	11	12	13	14
15	16	17	18	19	20	21
22	23	24	25	26	27	28
29	30	31	1	2	3	4

dia di trabou

workdays

MO	TU	WE	TH	FR	SA	SU
1	2	3	4	5	6	7
8	9	10	11	12	13	14
15	16	17	18	19	20	21
22	23	24	25	26	27	28
29	30	31	1	2	3	4

weekend

weekend

aña
year

awacero
rain
arco iris
rainbow
bientu
wind
sneeuw
snow
lente
spring
herfst
fall
zomer
summer
winter
winter

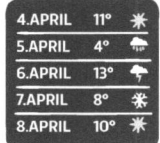

4.APRIL 11°
5.APRIL 4°
6.APRIL 13°
7.APRIL 8°
8.APRIL 10°

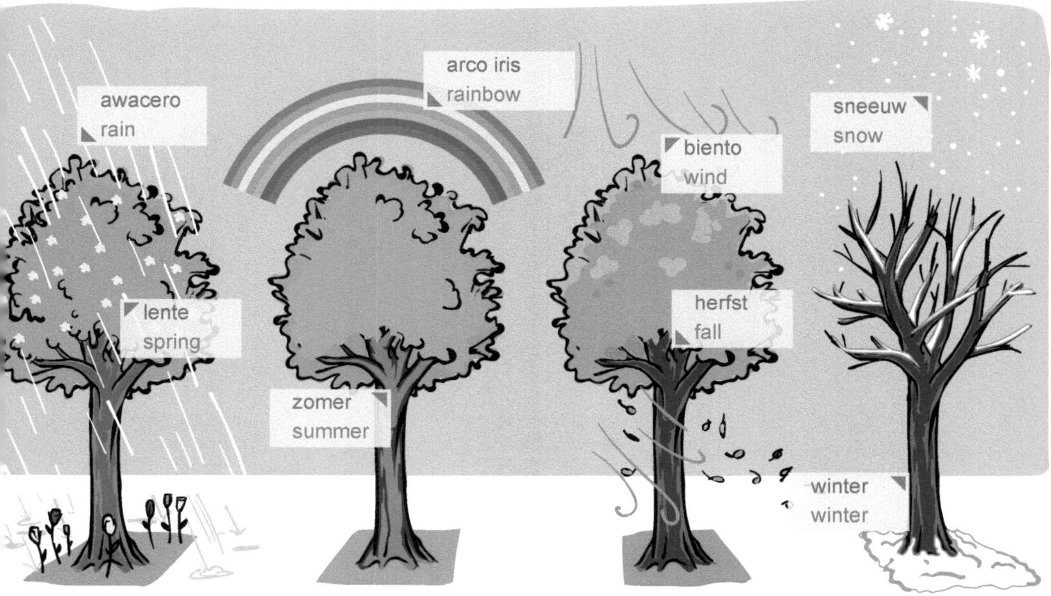

pronostico di tempo

weather forecast

F
C
120
90
60
30
0
-30
40
30
20
10
0
-10
-20

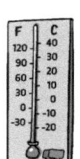

thermometer

thermometer

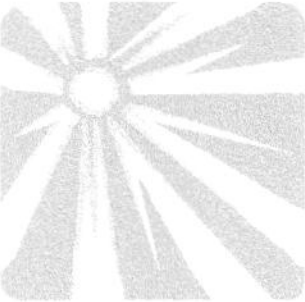

solo ta briya

sunshine

nubia

cloud

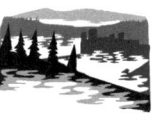

neblina

fog

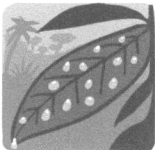

humedad

humidity

lamper

lightning

strena

thunder

mal tempo

storm

hagel

hail

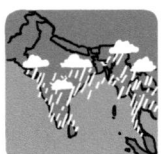

mal tempo

monsoon

inundacion

flood

ijs

ice

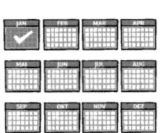

januari

January

februari

February

maart

March

april

April

mei

May

juni

June

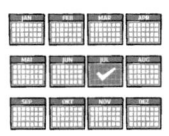

juli

July

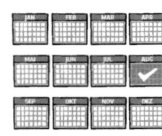

augustus

August

aña - year

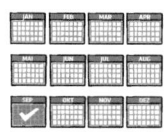

september
September

october
October

november
November

december
December

forma
shapes

circulo
circle

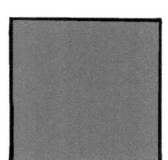

cuadra
square

rectangulo
rectangle

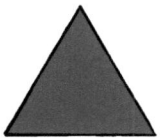

triangulo
triangle

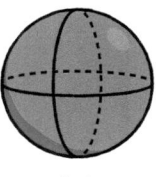

bol
sphere

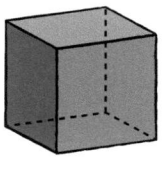

kubus
cube

blanco

white

geel

yellow

oraño

orange

ros

pink

cora

red

biña

purple

blauw

blue

berde

green

bruin

brown

shinishi

gray

preto

black

hopi / tiki

a lot / a little

rabia / trankil

angry / calm

bunita / mahos

beautiful / ugly

comienso / final

beginning / end

grandi / chikito

big / small

cla / scur

bright / dark

ruman homber / ruman muhe

brother / sister

limpi / sushi

clean / dirty

completo / incompleto

complete / incomplete

dia / anochi

day / night

morto / bibo

dead / alive

hancho / smal

wide / narrow

comibel / incomibel

edible / inedible

mal hende / bon hende

evil / kind

ansioso / ferfela bo mes

excited / bored

gordo / flaco

fat / thin

prome / ultimo

first / last

amigo / enemigo

friend / enemy

yen / bashi

full / empty

duro / moli

hard / soft

pisa / lihe

heavy / light

hamber / sed

hunger / thirst

malo / saludabel

ill / healthy

ilegal / legal

illegal / legal

inteligente / sabi

intelligent / stupid

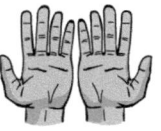

robes / drechi

left / right

cerca / leu

near / far

nobo / uza

new / used

nada / algo

nothing / something

bieu / jong

old / young

cendi / paga

on / off

habri / cera

open / closed

keto / duro

quiet / loud

rico / pober

rich / poor

bon / fout

right / wrong

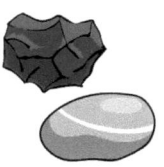

grof / liso

rough / smooth

tristo / contento

sad / happy

cortico / largo

short / long

pocopoco / lihe

slow / fast

muha / seco

wet / dry

cayente / friu

warm / cool

guera / paz

war / peace

contrario - opposites

0

cero

zero

1

un

one

2

dos

two

3

tres

three

4

cuater

four

5

cinco

five

6

seis

six

7

shete

seven

8

ocho

eight

9

nuebe

nine

10

dies

ten

11

diesun

eleven

12
diesdos
twelve

13
diestres
thirteen

14
diescuatro
fourteen

15
diescinco
fifteen

16
diesseis
sixteen

17
diesshete
seventeen

18
diesocho
eighteen

19
diesnuebe
nineteen

20
binti
twenty

100
shen
hundred

1.000
mil
thousand

1.000.000
miyon
million

idioma

languages

Ingles
....
English

Ingles Mericano
....
American English

Chines Mandarin
....
Chinese Mandarin

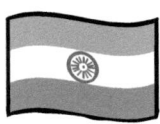

Hindi
....
Hindi

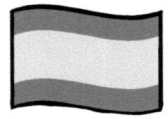

Spaño
....
Spanish

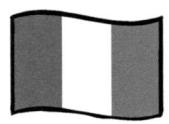

Frances
....
French

Arabe
....
Arabic

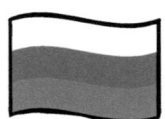

Ruso
....
Russian

Portugues
....
Portuguese

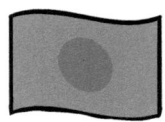

Bengal
....
Bengali

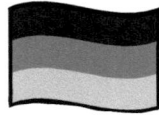

Aleman
....
German

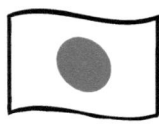

Hapones
....
Japanese

ami

I

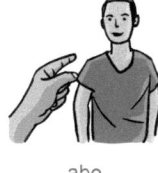

abo

you

e

he / she / it

nos

we

boso

you

nan

they

ken?

who?

kico?

what?

con?

how?

unda?

where?

ki ora?

when?

nomber

name

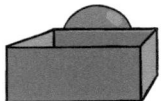

patras

behind

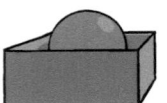

den

in

dilanti di

in front of

ariba

over

riba

on

bou di

under

banda di

beside

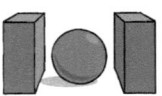

entre

between

luga

place